Senses

Smelling
in Living Things

Karen Hartley, Chris Macro and Philip Taylor

Heinemann
LIBRARY

First published in Great Britain by Heinemann Library,
Halley Court, Jordan Hill, Oxford OX2 8EJ
a division of Reed Educational and Professional Publishing Ltd.
Heinemann is a registered trademark of Reed Educational & Professional Publishing Ltd.

OXFORD MELBOURNE AUCKLAND
JOHANNESBURG BLANTYRE GABORONE
IBADAN PORTSMOUTH (NH) USA CHICAGO

Designed by Celia Floyd
Illustrated by Alan Fraser
Originated by Ambassador Litho Ltd, UK
Printed in Hong Kong / China

04 03 02 01 00
10 9 8 7 6 5 4 3 2 1

ISBN 0 431 09723 2

British Library Cataloguing in Publication Data

Hartley, Karen
    Smelling in living things. – (Senses)
    1. Smell – Juvenile literature
    2. Sense organs – Juvenile literature
    I. Title II. Macro, Chris III. Taylor, Philip
    573.8'77

Acknowledgements

The Publishers would like to thank the following for permission to reproduce photographs:

Ardea London: Ian Beames p.21; Bruce Coleman: Andrew Purcell p.29, Hans Reinhard p.22, Jane Burton p.28; Heinemann: Gareth Boden p.4, p.5, p.6, p.7, p.8, p.10, p.12, p.13, p.14, p.15, p.24, p.25, p.26, p.27; Image Bank: Paul McCormick p.18; Oxford Scientific Films: Frederick Ehrenstrom p.17; Pictor International p.20; Richard Greenhill p.11; Tony Stone: Daniel J Cox p.16, p.23, Kevin Summers p.19.

Cover photograph reproduced with permission of Oxford Scientific Films and Gareth Boden.

Many thanks to the teachers and pupils of Abbotsweld Primary School, Harlow.

Every effort has been made to contact copyright holders of any material reproduced in this book. Any omissions will be rectified in subsequent printings if notice is given to the Publisher.

For more information about Heinemann Library books, or to order, please telephone +44 (0)1865 888066, or send a fax to +44 (0)1865 314091. You can visit our web site at www.heinemann.co.uk

Any words appearing in the text in bold, **like this**, are explained in the Glossary.

Contents

What are your senses?

People and animals have senses to help them find out about the world. You use your senses to feel, see, hear, taste and smell. Your senses can warn you of danger.

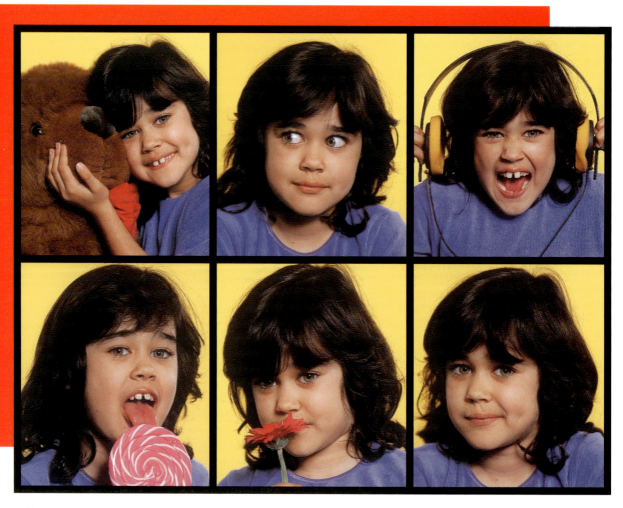

Your senses are very important to you and other animals every day. This book is about your sense of smell. You are going to find out how it works and what you use it for.

What do you use to smell?

You smell with your nose. That is the only place you can sense smells. Noses can be all sorts of different shapes and sizes but they all work in the same way.

Your nose has two small **nostrils** which are close to your mouth. The nostrils have many small hairs inside to stop you from breathing dust and grit in with the air.

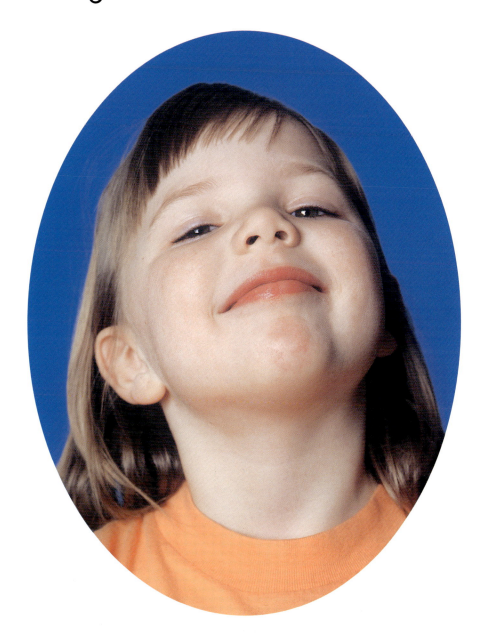

How does a nose work?

The smell of an orange is made up of very tiny pieces of the orange. They are too small to see or touch. They mix with the air that you breathe.

When you breathe in air, the smell of the orange goes up your nose too. It touches special smell **receptors** inside your head. These tell your brain what you are smelling.

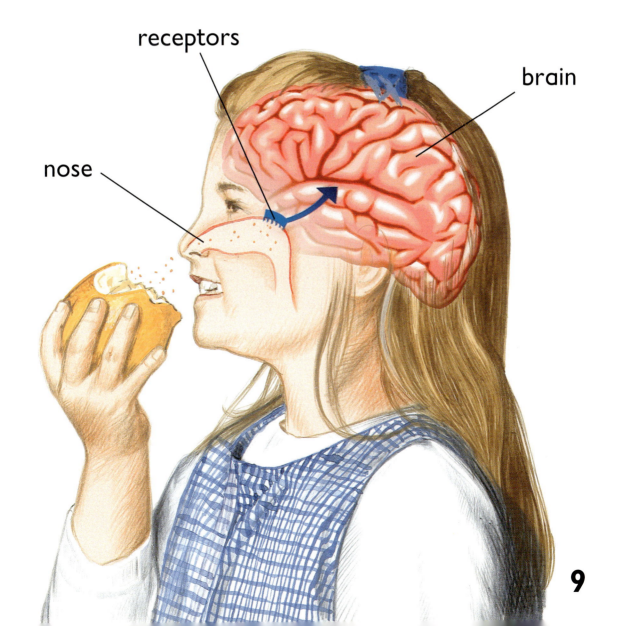

receptors

brain

nose

9

How does your nose help you?

Your sense of smell helps you to feel hungry when you need to eat. When you smell tasty food your mouth makes **saliva** to get ready for the meal.

Some smells let you know about things which are bad for you so you can move away from them. Some smells, like the smoke from fire, can warn you of danger nearby.

Using your nose

Your sense of smell tells you that your food is cooking and is nearly ready. You can also use smell to tell if it is cooked too much.

Your sense of smell also helps you to taste things better. It is the smell of your food in your nose that makes it seem so good and makes you want to eat it.

What can happen?

When you are ill with coughs, colds and **sinus** trouble your nose can get blocked. You cannot breathe very easily and you lose the sense of smell for a while.

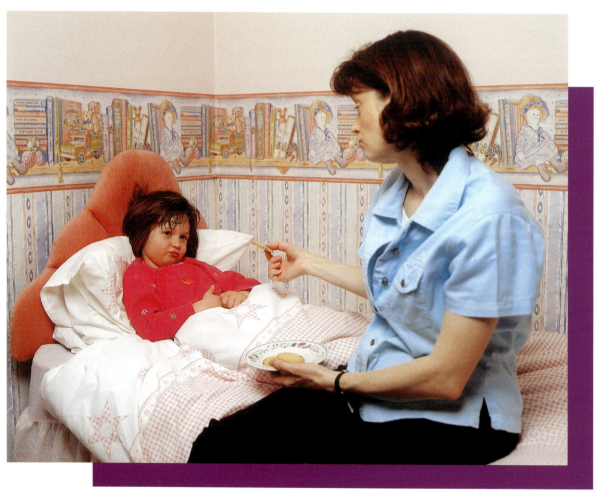

There are many special sweets, tablets and other **medicines** which can help to clear your nose. If you can smell things again you feel a bit better.

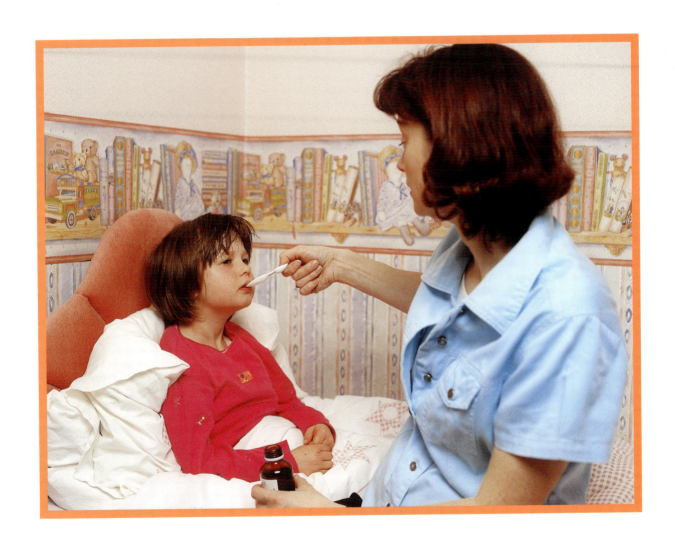

Do animals have noses?

Most animals have some way of sensing smells around them. Monkeys and **apes** have noses very much like yours. They work in just the same way.

Many fish have **nostrils** at the front of their heads. They breathe in the water as they swim. They can smell **scents** in the water.

Other ways to sense smells

Insects like bees have **feelers** with smell **receptors** at the ends. Some flowers have strong **scents**. The feelers sense the smell, and guide the bees to the flowers.

Snails have two pairs of feelers. They stretch the short ones out in front as they move. They use them to smell what is around them.

How do animals use smells?

Smelling is a very important sense for many animals. They use it to find food. Animals like dogs, foxes and snakes use their noses to find the animals which they like to eat.

Many animals **recognise** each other using smell. Ants have **feelers** which they can use to smell strangers. Only ants which smell like them are allowed in the nest.

Using smell to stay safe

Deer have a very good sense of smell. They can sniff the wind to smell danger. Fierce animals could be hunting them. The deer run away quickly to try to escape.

The skunk can make a very unpleasant smell when it is in danger. This nearly always stops its enemy from following it.

Investigating with your nose

How good is your sense of smell? Some flowers have stronger **scents** than others. Can you learn to **recognise** different types of flowers by the scent they make?

Ask someone to put some different foods into pots and cover them with cloth. Do not look inside. Can you guess what they are just by using your nose to smell them?

Playing tricks on your nose

If you cannot smell foods it is hard to tell the difference between them. Try holding your nose while someone puts a piece of raw onion on your tongue. Then try a piece of raw carrot. Is there a difference?

Sometimes smells can remind you of things you have done. The smell of shells and seaweed can remind you of holidays at the seaside.

Did you know?

Some fish have an amazing sense of smell. Trout like to eat shrimps. They can smell the **scents** from shrimps when they are a long way away.

Some **male** moths have a very strong sense of smell. They can recognise a **female** moth who is miles away. They have long complicated **feelers** which they use to smell.

Glossary

apes   animals like gorillas and chimpanzees

feelers   long thin growths on the heads of some small animals which help them to know what is around them

female   a girl

insects   small animals with six legs

male   a boy

medicines   special drugs that can help us to get better when we are ill

nerve   something that carries messages from the body to the brain

nostrils   holes in the nose with tubes going up into the head

receptors   tiny parts of bodies which can sense what is around them

recognise   to know what something is

saliva   the spit which wets our mouths when we are about to eat

scents   another word for smells

sinus   tiny tubes at the tops of your nostrils which go into your head

Sense map

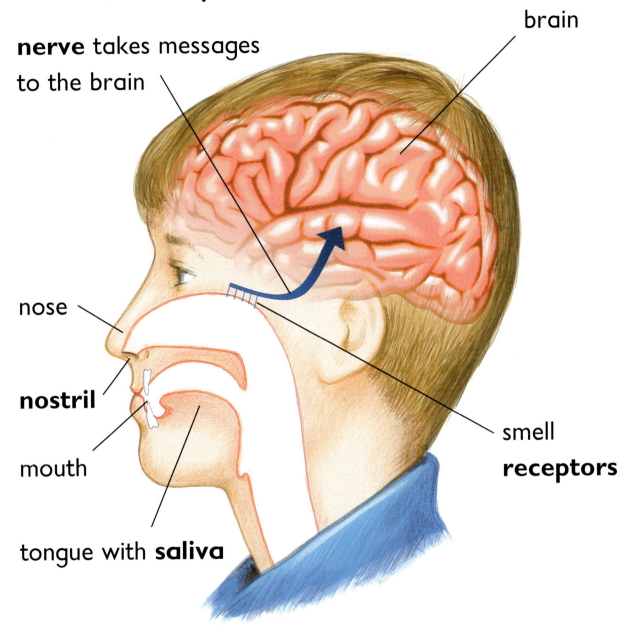

brain

nerve takes messages
to the brain

nose

nostril

mouth

tongue with **saliva**

smell
receptors

31

Index